# Veterinary Tales

## Jim Watkins

*Illustrated by Aongus Collins*

*Keeper*

**A Keeper original paperback**

First published in 2011
by

| Keeper |

an imprint of
Killaloe Communications
*www.killaloe.ie/khs*
*www.kllaloe.ie/kcs*

Trade enquiries to (061) 374656

A CIP record for this title is available from the National Library

Text © 2011: Jim Watkins

The author has asserted his moral rights

ISBN 978-1-907107-85-6
(original paperback)

Typeset in 14 point Bookman Old Style

*For
all the animals I treated
especially
the ones
that
never recovered
and
those that survived
in spite of me*

# Acknowledgements

MY heartfelt thanks to the Killaloe Hedge-School of Writing, where I learned so much about writing these stories; also to Anna Branagan, Wenda Arden, Niamh McKeogh, Prisca McNally, Jean Borreye and Kathleen Thorne who typed them for me; to David Rice who edited them; and to the members of the Ballina-Killaloe Writers' Circle for their constant encouragement. And to Aongus Collins for his superb illustrations.

# Foreword
## by David Rice

EVERY morning around six a tall figure can be seen collecting the debris left by the tourists and visitors to Ballina-Killaloe. This is Jim Watkins, whose Tidy Towns Committee, of which he is chairperson, has transformed the little town.

All through spring and summer the place is alive with flowers; the streets and roadways have signs which they never had before; there are now double-yellows lines where there should have been ones years ago. And everything is clean and tidy, thanks to that committee and Jim Watkins.

From his years of experience operating the pound for Dublin County Council, Jim knows exactly how to get along with local government – hence the double yellow lines and the street signs, and the speed bumps and much else that makes Ballina-Killaloe such a lovely place to live. We owe a lot to Jim Watkins and we are glad he chose Ballina-Killaloe to retire to.

He also happens to be a fascinating public speaker, and it was only natural that he was asked to become president of the local Toastmasters. It was there that people began to hear the tales of his more than five decades as a vet, and they simply kept urging him to write the stories down. Finally Jim gave in, and it turns out that he is as good a writer as he is a speaker.

These, then, are the tales from Jim's life as a vet – ordinary simple stories – with a few minor changes to protect the guilty. The tales can be funny, touching, sad, joyful, but all are true.

# Preface

I HAVE written these stories because I was persuaded by colleagues and many friends to do so. The era in which these events occurred was the Fifties. The location? Mainly the western half of the country and some locations in the east (as well as a brief spell in western Scotland). In that period — there were no televisions in the Republic; all the aircraft flying into Shannon were propeller-driven; rural electrification was only in its infancy; there were few cars on the road, and no speed restrictions.

Mobile phones were unknown; unemployment was rife; there were few industries outside of Dublin; women were not to be seen in pubs.

In one east-coast town in the great summer of 1955, a Garda road-block was established to stop women in shorts from a neighbouring holiday camp from entering the town.

Hard drugs were also unknown, regarded as something that happened in America only. Sean T. O'Kelly was President. There was no such thing as pub grub, and there were no supermarkets.

All the stories here are true in every detail; however some names have been changed to avoid embarrassment.

# A tale of
# the unexpected

I HAD never been to the small town on the Shannon before and I didn't know anyone there, not even the vet for whom I was going to do locum.

I mounted the green CIE bus in Dublin. It was a Leyland *Tiger* and it had a ladder up by the side of the rear window for access to a large box-like structure at the rear roof of the bus, for carrying luggage.

There were no bus stops so would-be passengers held out their hands anywhere on the road in order to stop the bus.

The conductor would dismount and load the luggage, which varied from suitcases to boxes of chickens and sacks of potatoes. Invariably the conductor would chat to people he knew on the route.

There was no hurry, however. The bus was noisy and everything from door to windows vibrated. It took most of the day to travel to the small town in the Midwest.

It arrived eventually and I suppose I was suffering from bus-lag. The term jet-lag was yet to come as only propeller planes flew into Shannon at that time.

The vet was anxious to get away to Rosses Point to play golf. He quickly showed me the instruments, drugs and the car. It was a Morris. I noted ominously the starting handle sticking out of the front of the engine. There was a girl who would take the phone calls and answer the door.

It was Saturday and the vet drove off with his wife, leaving me in charge.

No calls came in that evening and I proceeded to read the local newspaper. *Mrs O'Malley's cow had twins last Tuesday*, I read. *John O'Brien was fined 5/- for urinating on the Garda Barracks wall.*

There was no television in the Republic at this stage, so I went to bed at 11 p.m., happy that the next day was Sunday and shouldn't be a busy day.

At 6 a.m. the phone rang. I took down the name and address: it was a cow having difficulties calving.

I went to the car outside the door, turned the ignition key, swung the starting handle and the car started immediately.

I drove down the street and then it hit me. Where was I going? I hadn't a clue where the farm was so I decided to drive around the town to see if I could see someone going to early Mass.

I wasn't to know that the first Mass on Sundays in this sleepy town was at midday. Until 11.30 a.m. everyone was unconscious. I now had a choice of eight roads to travel; surely I must meet someone driving cows for early-morning milking.

I decided to take the first road to my left. I drove for one mile, two miles, three miles, and after four miles I decided to go back to the town.

I pulled into a gateway in order to turn and then I saw smoke rising straight up, as there was no wind. I drove in the gate and along an avenue and eventually after 50 yards or so the house came into view.

It was in a slight hollow – it was two storey on the right and single storey on the left.

I noted with delight that there was a man in the doorway of the single storey from whence came the smoke.  There were ten bikes leaning against the wall.

I drove straight to him and proffered the paper with the name and address. He took the paper and he held it.  I noticed he was swaying slightly; I got a strong whiff of alcohol.

'This is it,' he said with a laugh. 'This is it.'

I said 'What?'

'The cow's in the shed,' he said. 'I'll get you a bucket of water.'

I was astonished. There must have been hundreds of farms in the whole area and by a freak chance I had hit upon the very place where I was needed.

I donned my rubber apron and wellies, poured disinfectant in the bucket, washed the cow's rear, soaped my arm and entered the womb.  The calf was ready to come, a slight pull and he slid into my arms, kicking and spluttering.

There was nothing wrong at all.  The cow would have calved herself anyway.

I was very pleased and I returned to the house with the man who was smiling from ear to ear. I entered the kitchen. There were ten men there. Some were asleep in chairs; two were draped over the kitchen table. There were bottles of stout, half empty glasses and playing cards on the kitchen table. Must be a poker school, I thought.

'Ye must have had a hell of a session last night,' I remarked.

'Certainly did,' a bleary-eyed man answered.

Someone touched my elbow. I turned: it was an elderly woman.

'How is the cow?' she asked.

'You have a baby son,' I said gleefully.

'Would you like to see the boss?' she asked.

'Certainly,' I replied, thinking to myself, *I'm going to get paid.*

I followed her into the other half of the house and surprisingly up the stairs. She pushed open a door into one of the bedrooms and in a flash I took in the starched white sheets, the flickering candles and the withered corpse of an old man! I had stumbled on a wake. The men

in the kitchen were neighbours who were keeping the widow company for the night.

I think I almost collapsed with the shock.   I turned to the old woman.' I'm sorry,' I said. 'I didn't know – I only arrived in town yesterday.'

I said a quick prayer and left, still stunned by the whole series of events. Was it a coincidence or was it an unseen hand that guided me to that house?

Last year I was in the town with my niece.   I had often told her the story and she was dying to see where the events had taken place.  We drove the same road, one mile, two miles, three miles and four miles, I entered the gateway and drove in.

Alas, there wasn't a stone left where the house once stood. I felt rather sad.

# The butler

I DON'T suppose that there are as many stately homes now as there were in the 1950s. I mean Victorian or Georgian mansions with a retinue of servants, butlers and chauffeurs.

In those years I worked as a student with Patrick who was a vet on an east coast town. Many of our customers were near the sea and this was very handy in the hot summer of 1955, especially after dirty jobs like afterbirth removals, of which there were plenty of cases.

Pat and I would dash into the sea in a secluded place and out again to get rid of the afterbirth smell.

Sometimes we wore togs and sometimes not. On one occasion we were just

returning to the car when we heard giggling, and to our horror we discovered that a large group of girl guides were camped just around the headland and had seen us–this time we had no togs!

Pat said it didn't matter since we were too far away to be recognised. However, one of our calls brought us to the stately home.

Ornamental gates and a tree-lined avenue led to a fork in the avenue with a sign *Private visitors* to the left and *Tradesmen* to the right. We looked at each other and grinned and took the tradesman's entrance.

We arrived in the yard at the rear of the house. A stable door was open and there was a jersey cow recumbent. She had calved the night before. Pat made the diagnosis of milk fever and administered the calcium injection which was the treatment.

Most cows respond very rapidly to the treatment but some require further treatment. We got a call again to the same cow the very next day. On each occasion it was the butler in morning suit who met us. He always had a clean towel draped over his left arm with a bar of soap in his hand and a basin of hot water in his right. He held it there while we washed after treating the cow.

Again the cow appeared to get better but the next day she was still recumbent. This time the butler announced that Miss Frances would like to interview both of us. I declined, as I was a student, but the butler insisted and so I went.

Paddy still wore his wellingtons as his shoes were back in the surgery. The butler led the way through a large kitchen, with giggling maids, up several flights of stairs to a large sitting room.

Madame was seated to the right of the marble fireplace and her husband, who seemed very old and doddery, sat to the left.

Beside Madame there was an umbrella stand which contained many walking sticks with silver handles and also shooting sticks and umbrellas as well. Madame introduced her husband who nodded but I don't think he was too interested.

Paddy started to explain to Madame about the milk fever, its causes and treatment... The woman asked a lot of questions.

In the midst of this I became aware of a little dog; I think it was a shi-tzu. It had fastened itself onto Paddy's boot and was trying to make love to it.

I bit my lip to stop myself from laughing. Paddy never batted an eyelid but continued talking about milk fever. I knew he couldn't kick the dog away for fear of giving offence.

Madame never batted an eyelid either. Without saying a word, she deftly removed a long thin cane from the umbrella stand. I can still hear the whistle as it slashed through the air to impact on the dog's rump. The little dog jumped, it seemed, three feet into the air and the screeches were ear-shattering. He shot out of the door, still screeching. The screeches continued as he descended the many stairs but with diminished intensity.

When we came back down to the yard the cow was standing at last – the butler was smiling all over his face.

Paddy and I laughed all the way back to the surgery.

# The ghost

I HAD known Kevin at boarding school. He was captain of the winning Leinster Schools Cup Team one year, so everyone in the school knew him.

He was big in every sense – and quiet and gentle off the field.

Sadly about two years after leaving school he was killed playing rugby. An accidental kick in the head lead to something more serious and he died.

I was not aware of this for a long time as he lived a long way from Dublin. Years later I arrived in a town in the North West to do locum for an ageing vet. I lived in with the vet and his wife in a beautiful location, the house overlooked the Shannon.

When I went to my bedroom the first evening I noted the pictures of rugby teams and was surprised that they were all from my old school. Kevin was in them all.

The vet I was working for was also called Kevin so I assumed he was the father of Kevin the rugby star.

Next morning at breakfast I asked my boss and he was delighted that I had known Kevin junior, as he was indeed his son. After breakfast he took me to the local cemetery and showed me the grave. On the way back he reminisced about Kevin junior and told me I was sleeping in his room and that's why the rugby photos were there.

That night in the room I couldn't stop thinking about Kevin junior. The adulation he received as captain of the winning rugby team and now so young and no longer in this world. His remains are in the ground about one mile from his home.

One night about 2 a.m. I was awakened by a noise in the room. I put on the bedside lamp but there was nothing there to account for the noise. I went back to sleep.

Three nights later, this time at 4.30 a.m., I awoke again to the noise. It was a kind of rustle cum dragging noise like something being dragged over the floor.

Again there was nothing.

Next morning I said to the boss, 'I think there's a mouse in my room.'

He immediately told me that there were no mice in the house, let alone in my room. Nevertheless he gave me a mouse-trap and some cheese. I set the trap but after a few days I noted the dust on the trap and the mould growing on the cheese. The boss was right: there were no mice!

The noise occurred again from time to time, still with no fixed schedule – just at various hours of the night.

Eventually I slept with the light on and one morning I woke to find the light had gone out – no, a ghostly hand hadn't switched it off – the bulb had blown.

This situation continued for some weeks and it was beginning to get on my nerves.

One day I got a call to a place I had never heard of and I went to my room to look at a rather detailed local map. While I was looking at the map I heard the noise – I whipped around and caught the culprit.

Each night before I went to bed I had opened the window. Sometimes in the night a breeze off the Shannon would billow the lace curtains. However these were too long and dragged along the floor, catching in bumps in the wood. This created the dragging sound which was like a sack (with a body in it) being pulled along.

I slept soundly after this episode.

# Directions

FINDING one's way to a client in unknown territory could be a problem. There was a chronic lack of sign-posting, along with a scarcity of people on the roads, particularly in Leitrim. And in wintertime darkness added to the problem.

People would hold out a left hand and tell you to turn right. Others would say they never heard of the client – that would be because I didn't know his nickname. In some places there were so many people of the same name that they all had nicknames.

Very often if I stopped someone they would look in the back of the VW and see the veterinary equipment. They would then ask, 'Are you the vet?'

Then they might start a conversation about anything at all and keep on talking until you said, 'Excuse me, I have an urgent call to.....'

One man asked me where I was from. When I said Dublin, he said, 'Do you know Clontarf?'

'Of course,' I said.

'D'ye know Maurice McGowan, at all?'

'I do,' I lied.

He was delighted.

'He's a cousin of mine,' he said with pride.

The man thought Dublin was a village – he had never been outside Mayo in his whole life. What a culture shock it would have been for him to see Dublin.

One frosty night I got totally lost. I got out of the car at a remote crossroads. I turned 360 degrees, there was not a light to be seen. I recall the wind moaning over the bog, and the starry sky. It was a lonely kind of feeling. I drove on.

Suddenly in the corner of my eye I saw a movement in the ditch. I stopped and got out.

I said, 'Hello.' There was no answer.

I could vaguely see two heads in the ditch.

I said, 'Look, I'm totally lost. Will you please help me?'

The man sheepishly came out of the dyke; the girl crouched down. He looked at the ground and sent me to the client's house, which was quite near.

The animals were large pigs with swine erysipelas. A shot of penicillin each should fix them. The farmer had a tilly lamp which was faulty. We had to catch each large pig individually, inject and then mark him with dye so we wouldn't inject him twice. Each time the lamp died down, the pigs would run in to chew my boots. It wasn't the pigs I was afraid of. It was the rats! I suppose it was a great source of food for rats in this very lonely place. I was glad to leave.

Another time in daylight I enquired and got directions from two men on bikes. 'Down that road and it's the first new house on your right. You can't miss it,' they both said.

I drove for two miles and came to a T-junction. I met a man leading an ass. The ass had panniers on his back filled with turf.

'You've passed it,' he said, 'Turn around, and it'll be the first new house on your left.'

Puzzled, I drove back. I couldn't understand how I could have missed a new house.

About half the way back a man waved me down.

'Are you the vet?'

'Yes.'

'I'm the man that's expecting you.'

'Oh good. Where's this new house?'

'That's it,' he said, pointing.

'Gosh,' I said. 'When was that built?'
'In 1926.'

All the other houses on the road were from the 1830s and 40s, and so this was known as 'the New House' ever after.

On at least one occasion the boss and I went to an out-farm on instructions from the owner to treat a lame cow. The farmer didn't come with us, but gave us directions to get to the out-farm. We found 30 cows tied in a shed. The problem was to find out which cow it was.

Eventually, after being kicked and pucked by almost all the cows, we decided one cow had a funny-looking hoof. We trimmed the horn of the hoof. The sweat pumped out of us, my boss growling, 'Next time, I'll make damned sure the owner comes with us.'

I was sore and tired after holding up several cows' legs while the boss examined them.

We discovered later that we were at the wrong farm.

Years later I called to a house to vaccinate a dog. The owner was away at work, but he said the dog would be found tied to a tree in the back garden.

The dog turned out to be a very large,

extremely unfriendly German shepherd. Eventually I managed to vaccinate him, after a grim struggle in which my trousers were ripped.

Again, it was the wrong house! So much for directions!

# The digs

WHEN doing locums in the country one sometimes stayed in the vet's house, but for the most part it would be a local house. The term *B&B* was not used in those days.

The accommodation varied greatly, as did the food.

*En Suite* was never on the cards. I arrived on one occasion to a village in the south of the country to a friendly welcome from the landlady. She told me she had managed a hotel in London before she was married. I looked forward to a satisfactory stay in this 'digs'.

On the first day I was very busy indeed and by evening time I was starving. The bread and butter, tea and two bananas did little to alleviate the situation.

The watery 'stew' the following day was not much better. The woman hadn't a clue how to cook and I doubted her claim to have been in any hotel. I tried to eat out as far as possible.

The same digs housed a garda, a forestry official and a bulldozer driver.

As the digs was also a pub, there was heavy drinking on weekends and after hours some of the drinkers would repair to the kitchen. The garda, whose nickname was 'High Noon' because of his resemblance to Gary Cooper, would join in the after-hours drinking. One morning I came down to breakfast to find the forester in High Noon's uniform, and High Noon naked on the couch!

In another digs the landlady never let me inside until I had deposited my boots or shoes in a box outside the door – I would then don slippers inside the house. If anyone left shoes under their bed, the shoes would be parcelled and placed on top of the wardrobe!

There was a superb vegetable garden around the house which was carefully tended by the woman's husband. The vegetables were sold and every day we got a kind of stuffing made of onion, bread, thyme and parsley as a replacement vegetable.

The next digs was also a pub. On the first night, having put my luggage in the bedroom (which had seen better days), I was looking for the bathroom. The proprietor pointed me in the direction of the back yard. A structure had been erected but never finished. Four walls and spaces for the windows and door but these were lacking. So too was the roof. There was a flush loo but the lack of a proper foundation meant that only the rim of the bowl was visible. This loo was also used by the people in the bar and at night many put their feet into the bowl as there was no light!

When I arrived the proprietor had been handling flour in the grocery part of the pub. I noticed floury fingerprints on my luggage – I reckon it was just curiosity, as there was nothing missing.

In the middle of the bar there was a constant dribble of rain from a leaking roof, so most of the customers sat on stools in the adjoining kitchen where there was a turf fire.

At the table where I ate, there was always a little child crawling noisily around the floor. Sometimes his hand would come over the edge of the table into my potatoes.

The teapot would be left near the turf fire to draw and, before the kitchen girl withdrew it to pour the tea, she would blow a great puff at it to get rid of the turf dust.

The men were very friendly and when I came first they tried to guess where I came from by my accent.

One night a number of men spent all night drinking in the pub. They left early the next morning to go out some miles to dig a grave for a neighbour. I saw the funeral cortege go out at 3 p.m. in a snow-storm. It came back, plus coffin, at 4 p.m. The men had dug the wrong grave.

Another digs was, in fact, a rather run-down hotel, part of which was also an undertakers. It was infested with mice and I could hear them scratching in the night.

Our surgery was a small room next to the coffin-house and the operating table was a rusty barrel on which we put news-paper when operating.

We ate out in a local restaurant rather than the hotel.

One Easter weekend, I discovered that Barney, the hearse man who was also a barman in the hotel, was going to St. Vincent's in Dublin to pick up the body of a local man who had died there. I cadged a lift as I wanted to be home for Easter. The deceased's brother accompanied us – he was already quite drunk and frequently begged the driver to stop at various pubs. Barney did not, wisely, as we would never have reached Dublin.

We went down a side street to the side door of the morgue. I bade farewell to the driver and started up the lane. A rather tough-looking nurse caught me by the arm. 'Where do you think you're going?'

'I'm going home,' I replied.

'Not before you give us a hand. We're short of staff.'

First she handed me a bag containing the deceased's clothes and shoes, which I put in the hearse. Then she beckoned me in. The idea was that the driver and I were to lift the awful-looking corpse into the coffin. I took the feet and Barney took the shoulders. We did it. I thought I would never get out of the place.

One time I arrived to work for a vet in the northern-half of the country.

As I stepped from the car two men caught me by the arms.

'Now, Mr. Hetherington,' one said, 'we're arresting you under Section (I can't remember) and you'll be charged with abandonment of your wife and child, defrauding the Revenue Commissioners, etc.'

'I'm afraid you've made a bad mistake here,' I said. 'Look at my driving licence – it's in the glove compartment. I'm not Hetherington and I'm not married either.'

One of them looked in the glove compartment whilst the other held on to me. Eventually they apologised and let me go. Hetherington was to have done work for the vet but had failed to turn up – I had got the job instead.

Just then my employer arrived and I explained the situation. He told the detectives about Hetherington but, since he had never seen him and he only knew me from the previous day, I was again arrested.

Following a phone call to my local sergeant in Dublin I was eventually set free.

My ordeal was not yet over, as the following day I drove into the yard and another man pounced on me. He was a tax official. I drove him to the Garda station and managed to find one of my detective friends, who laughingly assured the tax official that I was not Hetherington.

One hotel I stayed in was run by two women. One night they called me into their office. I didn't know until then that there was a spy hole which looked into the residents' lounge. They asked me if I recognised anyone. I did. There was Robert, a neighbour of mine from home. I was delighted to see him and I thought it was nice of the women to tell me.

Alas, their motivation was not what I thought. 'Is that his wife?' one of the women asked.

'Oh, gosh, yes, of course,' I lied.

Robert was a notorious womaniser and, if I had told the truth, he would not have been allowed to stay the night in *that* hotel.

Some of the commercial reps who stayed in the hotel were always playing tricks on one another. Since most bedrooms were supplied with chamber pots, a favourite trick was to place a pot outside someone's door, fill it with red lemonade and throw in a few sausages. The maid

who serviced the rooms would be shocked
and the occupier embarrassed.

# Hair today, gone tomorrow

DID YOU ever hear of Mr Christy of London? No? Well, years ago this man used to take a half-page ad in the Sunday papers, advertising his cure for baldness.

There were three of us in the digs. Bill, the bank cashier, John, who worked in the local hardware and myself, assistant to the local vet.

As I got up first in the mornings I always brought in the post and so I couldn't help noticing the letters with the printed logo *Christy of London*. These letters were all for John.

One day I said to John, 'I couldn't help noticing the letters from Christy of London.'

'Yes,' he said, 'sadly, as you can see,

I'm going bald real fast and I'm scared I'll never get married. I've already spent £100 on these bottles from Christy, and nothing has happened.'

Now £100 was an enormous sum in those days and John could ill afford it. I advised him to spend no more and he agreed.

That night I took down one of my veterinary books and, along with John, I looked up *alopecia* – in animals of course but, as the causes and treatment were much the same in humans, I thought we might find something to help. The causes were listed as —

iodine deficiency;

dietary deficiency;

fleas, lice, mange and ringworm;

continued application of chemicals or irritants to the hair and skin;

advanced pregnancy in horses, sheep and dogs!

As John wasn't pregnant and didn't have fleas, lice, mange or ringworm, these were ruled out of his case.

Firstly, we purchased iodized salt for John, which we all began using as it gave a nice flavour to our dinners. John's fruit and vegetable intake was increased. After a month he looked great, but the hair didn't grow.

One day I visited the local chemist. He enquired, 'How is John? Is he still worried about that hair problem?'

Apparently John called regularly to see if there was anything new on the market for his problem.

The chemist mused, 'If only I could find that old book, it contained a formula which worked sometimes.'

The book had been published in the 1880s so I didn't hold out much hope even if he did find it. But find it he did and he phoned me and asked me to call to the shop.

When I called and looked at the ingredients I only recognised one or two of the chemical substances. The rest I had never heard of. However, I wrote up to Boilean & Boyd in Christchurch Place in Dublin but they did not have them. Instead they referred me to a London wholesaler who might have them in stock. They did, and in a few weeks a parcel arrived with powder, tablets, and a liquid tar-like substance.

John was aware of all this and was awaiting, with not a little excitement, the testing of the product (with him as guinea pig).

On the following Saturday night, at the rear of the chemist shop, the chemist and I pounded the tablets to powder in a mortar and pestle. We then boiled the tarry stuff and mixed the lot. We filled an old gallon wine jar with what looked like bog water with black streaks through it.

I returned to the digs and Billy and I washed John's hair, after which we liberally applied the newly-manufactured 'hair restorer'.

An area of John's head was examined with a lens and the approximate number of hairs was counted in a square inch on his scalp.

Each week until the solution was exhausted we repeated the process. Of course, the examination with the lens continued and we always reported new growth of one or two new hairs each week. This was part of our psychological warfare. The jokes during all this were hilarious and John joined in this, being the great guy that he was (and still is).

During this period John told me that he had to move 300 gas cylinders in the hardware store because there was an odour of a dead mouse. The mouse was never found, but John's assistant, who was moving the cylinders, eventually concluded that the odour was from John's head!

Unfortunately, his hair did not grow. However, John didn't *lose* any more of his hair and he has the same amount of hair now as he had then. He is married now for years, has a grown up family and is retired.

The loss of hair didn't make any difference to his life as he was promoted to be in charge of the hardware department in the company head office in Galway city.

He eventually had his own hardware business which he ran successfully until his retirement. He remains, after fifty years, a firm friend.

# The out farm

AN 'out farm' is a piece of land owned or rented by a farmer, but which is located some distance from the home farm. It would not be a popular destination for the vet, as usually there were few facilities such as cattle chutes, sheds or water for washing .

When John told me he had a heifer on an out farm in the hills which had a large lump under her eye and that she was pretty wild, I was full of foreboding. However, we made an arrangement to meet at an appointed time at the out farm. I had told him to have adequate help, so there were three men, himself and, of course, me.

There was an old abandoned thatched house with mud walls on the site and this was where we would capture and treat the animal. The four men disappeared up the hill and after a long while a herd of cattle thundered down eyes bulging, snorting and panting. No way would they enter the house even though the men did their best to force them in. Suddenly, the herd turned and raced back up the hill knocking down one of the men who tried to block them. The location was very isolated and rarely would these animals have seen a human being, which is why they were so wild.

Another appointment was made and this time a corral had been erected around the house. There were also two extra men, and we at last got the cattle into the house.

With my trusty scalpel in my hand I entered the maelstrom of heifers galloping around inside and eventually my quarry passed close to me. As she did I made a slash at the enormous swelling. It opened, disgorging the pussy contents of the abscess.

My success was short lived. Several of the animals tried to escape through the rear windows. These windows were narrower than the animals and, with the pressure exerted, the rear wall fell out and the roof fell on us, knocking us all to the ground. Blinded by the dust I scrambled to my feet, covered with straw and dust, and so did the other men, cursing and swearing as they struggled from the debris.

Simultaneously, we all felt the squiggling and heard the squeaking in our shirts and pants. There had been thousands of mice in the thatch and as we stood up they were struggling to escape from inside our clothing.

When it was all over we could do nothing but laugh.

*Jim Watkins*

# *The cars*

THE Volkswagen was the greatest thing to hit the veterinary profession. It was reliable, could be driven through the fields, and required no water so was sure to start even in severe frost. It was fast and economical.

The one I was supplied with in North Tipperary had huge mileage on the clock. As I worked every day from 8.30 a.m. to 11 p.m., I put enormous additional mileage on it. Not once did I have an engine failure.

However, there were some shortcomings. The horn didn't work; there were no brake lights or rear lights; only one headlamp functioned; the brakes were well worn and the steering questionable.

I never got a puncture – just blow-outs. The wheel nuts were self-locking and, on one occasion, while trying to loosen them, I stood on the wheel brace which bent under my weight. The garage man said that I should carry a hammer to tap the nuts with before using the wheel brace. This was certainly an improvement, but still hard work.

In the summer I didn't use the lights, except late at night, so the one headlamp was not a problem. When the nights got dark it was another story. The boss was always 'going to get something done about it' but it never happened.

Then one dark night, just outside the town, there were two of the biggest gardai I ever saw with their hands up to halt me.

The younger one walked to the driver's side, taking his notebook out as he did so.

'I've been watching you for some time,' he said. 'No tax disc displayed.'

He put his hand on the horn.

'No horn, bald tyres, no rear lights, *one* headlamp.'

I didn't volunteer the information about the brakes or the steering.

I had a vision of a dressing down in

the local court room from the district justice, a heavy fine, and headlines in the local paper. It would give the locals something to chuckle about.

The other garda – a sergeant – walked around the car, shining his torch into the back. He then shone the torch on me and said, 'Oh, it's the vet. My cow is in great nick after that job you did the other night.'

Suddenly, I recognised the figure. I had indeed stitched his cow's udder after she went through a barbed wire fence. On that occasion he was in his civvies.

'Tis all right, Mick,' he said to the other garda. 'Go on vet. And get that tax fixed up!'

When I told the boss he taxed the car at last, but nothing else was done.

One weekend I was driving home in heavy rain near Portlaoise; it was getting dusk. I put on my single light. Way ahead I saw a garda standing on the side of the road. I tried to hide behind the car in front but to no avail. The garda ran to his bicycle, which was parked on the hedge. He removed the lamp from the front of the bike and started to turn the screw on the top in order to light the lamp. Well, if he was screwing until Christmas it just wouldn't light and I flashed by him, boot to the floor at 70 mph, showering him with muddy spray!

The Morris Minor I had in Galway was a lovely car to drive, although not quite as rugged as the VW. Changing a wheel was, however, a dirty job. The jack was a vertical object with a hole in the middle; a bar was put into this and rotated. As the jack was well greased one finished up with greasy hands and, according to Murphy's Law, one's nose always got itchy at that point.

One evening I got a puncture on a bog road – I inserted the jack and commenced rotating. It worked all right except the jack kept going into the bog road (downwards) instead of upwards!

Some men came along and held up the car while I changed the wheel. I had to borrow a pickaxe to retrieve the jack out of the road.

Another problem with the Morris Minor was the fan belt: it would break over a certain mileage. So, acting on a tip-off from the garage man, I always carried a woman's nylon stocking as a spare. Eventually, the fan belt would give way and the nylon stocking worked extremely well.

In another practice, as the vet had crashed his VW, I was supplied with his sister's Ford Anglia. The car had to get oil in the engine every day and left an enormous smokescreen everywhere we went. Over 40 mph the car swayed from side to side and I was always afraid it would fall on its side. There were only two doors and these opened to the front, so if the wind caught the door when you opened it, you could get pulled out on to the road. And even if not, you'd have to get out of the car to retrieve the door from near the back bumper.

For no apparent reason there was a perfectly round hole in the floor in front of the passenger seat. On wet days the muck and rain would shoot in through the hole and hit the roof. It would then drip down on the seat. I tried covering up the hole with paper, but the wind would blow it aside.

One wet day a farmer's wife asked me for a lift into town. I warned her about the hole in the floor but she was determined to get to the town.

Eventually, she dismounted from the

car, bade me farewell and, as she walked away, I noticed a perfect circle of muck on her coat!

# Cyril

SOME of the vets I worked for also employed a workman. These men had many roles, like gardening or helping where there might be large numbers of cattle to be TB tested or dehorned. Of course, one or two of the vets had farms so their employees did general farm work like mending fences, cutting hedges and so on.

Cyril was such a man, but he was more. He was an exceedingly clever man.

In those days the profession of Veterinary Nurse did not exist but, if it had, Cyril would have qualified easily. He was a very keen observer of everything and had an incredible knowledge of diseases, drugs and various techniques.

I was amazed to find that he could

give a cow an epidural anaesthetic.

Sometimes when I was examining an animal I would make a diagnosis and when I turned to get the required drugs from the car, Cyril would be standing behind me with the very drugs in his hand. He would have made his own diagnosis. The boss used to make jokes about Cyril setting up in opposition to us.

The only thing I found annoying about Cyril was his laugh – it was more of a high-pitched kind of snigger. The boss said it was like a female gnu in the mating season. You'd hear it if you slipped and fell in the cow shed, or if you broke a syringe – this happened occasionally, as all syringes had glass barrels. Some sheds were so dark and, especially in Mayo, had a loft over the cows where turkeys and hens roosted. I used to forget about this until a defecation landed on my nose or a turkey jumped down on my head. Cyril would snigger away at this but, as he was such a great help, I said nothing.

One day the boss announced that he was going to Dublin on the train for a few days. He had just taken delivery of a brand new VW. I would be using this while he was away. I was terrified I might scratch it, so I was very careful driving in and out of farms and down the narrow boreens.

One very dark, wet night I was returning alone from a call in a rather lonely place when without warning a large horse came backwards out of a side boreen. His front leg was tied to his back leg so that he wouldn't be inclined to wander. I braked hard, the horse got a fright also and he fell backwards onto the front left wing, crumpling it dreadfully. The headlamp, still lighting, hung forlornly on its wiring. I surveyed the damage with shock – the horse having disappeared in the dark.

I drove slowly back to the vet's yard, wondering would they believe what had happened? How was I going to deal with this? The boss would die if he saw his new car. Would I go for the dealer and pay for it myself? What would it cost? And then I thought of Cyril. He'll know someone who'll fix it for a reasonable sum.

I searched the town and I found Cyril playing darts in one of the pubs.

'Cyril, I'm in trouble,' I said, telling him what had happened. 'Can you help me?'

'I can,' said he with a grin.

When he saw the car the high pitched snigger was the loudest I had heard him make.

'I'll fix it,' he said. 'You go to bed.'

I went to bed and gave him the car keys. I lay awake for a long time worrying about the whole affair but fell asleep eventually.

In the morning I hardly ate any breakfast. I looked out the top window. There was what looked like a brand new VW parked in front of the garage. I walked out and looked inside it. There were all the veterinary medicines, stomach tubes etc. It was the same car of the night before. The wing was perfect – I decided it must be a brand new wing and wondered what it would cost. Cyril arrived grinning. He told me it was the same wing. He had watched the lads in the local garage at work and he had got a loan of some equipment, with which he had beaten out the wing. He did not look for, nor would he accept, any remuneration, However, before I moved on to the next practice I rewarded him handsomely.

# Romy

IT WAS her clothes I noticed first. Not many women had hat, coat, gloves, and boots all with mink panels. I had worked on a mink farm. I valued them at between £4,000 and £5,000. My companion, who was a company accountant, was sure she was from Dublin – he thought he knew her face. I doubted this very much because we were in Hamburg Airport and we were about to fly to Paris.

We had been purchasing pharmaceuticals and were now going to visit another office in Paris. We arrived at the airport at 8.30 in the morning, but the flight was postponed several times due to severe weather conditions – it was snowing heavily on and off. The young woman of the mink panels arrived about noon, and it later transpired that she had been phoning the airport and was told that the flight would be leaving some time after that.

She was seated on the opposite side of the lounge facing us and presently she was joined by what I can only describe as 'the king of the hippies'. His hair was waist length and huge earrings jangled from his ears. He had a number of necklaces around his neck and the rest of his clothing was indescribable.

I wondered what the connection was. Could he be her husband, lover or friend? Suddenly the woman stood up and walked straight towards me. She stood in front of me and to my surprise she said in English, 'Do you mind if I sit beside you?'

I said, 'Not at all, but what about your friend?'

'Oh, that man? I don't know him; he's just a pest.'

We started to talk, where are you from, and so on. She told me she lived in Paris and had been working in Hamburg. I told her my story and when she heard I was from Ireland she said she'd love to go there someday, she'd heard so much about it.

My accountant, on the other side, whispered in my ear. 'She's from Dublin, I'm telling you. I've seen her before.'

I whispered back, 'She couldn't be. She has a continental accent and lives in Paris.'

At about 3.30 the snow stopped and the runway cleared and we started to move towards the boarding exit. At this stage the young woman asked me if I would please sit beside her as she didn't want to encounter the hippy again. I agreed and received a knowing look from the accountant.

On the way to Paris the woman and I chatted about many things. As we neared our descent into Paris the woman asked me if I had a place to stay there. (Actually, I had arranged to stay with a relative who worked in the OECD.)

To my surprise she said, 'Oh, you can come and stay with me.'

I said, 'I can't. I have the company accountant with me.'

'Oh, he can come too,' she said. 'I have a large apartment.'

Well, I had arranged beforehand to stay with my relative and he was expecting me. I thanked her and declined the offer.

Photo courtesy Engelbert Reineke/Wikimedia Commons

At the conveyor belt, still chatting, I noticed a number of people staring at us, especially the airport staff.

Eventually I bade farewell to Madame and then I asked one of the airport staff why they were staring, and he replied in a surprised manner, 'But, Monsieur, do you mean to tell me you don't know? That was Romy Schneider.'

I had vaguely heard the name before but, as I'm not a film fan, it didn't mean anything to me. Romy was in fact huge within the film world in Europe and was most famous for her roles in the *Sissi* films of the 1950s era. In later years she appeared with Peter Sellers and Peter O'Toole in *What's New Pussycat?* and many other films.

But there was more. Her mother, also an actress, had been a friend of Adolf Hitler. She used to visit him at the Berghof, accompanied by her child Romy, who played with Martin Bormann's children while there.

Sadly, Romy had a very tragic life, plagued by marriage break-ups. Her son was killed by falling onto spiked railings at his grandparents' home.

In 1962 Romy died suddenly. There was considerable speculation as to whether it was suicide. She is buried in Paris.

# The gates

AFTER several visits to Newton's I knew why my employer was reluctant to go there on sick calls. It wasn't just that the animals were invariably moribund and every quack cure available had been used on them. Neither was it the battleaxe who waited in the cobbled yard to abuse me for not coming fast enough, or would demand to know why the Boss himself hadn't come.

No, it was the Gates. The farm had been a landed gentry's estate and all the fields on the way in ran parallel to the road. You first had to open the imposing wrought-iron gate at the entrance, drive the car through, go back and close the gate, the follow a track that led through a meadow to the next gate. The next field was the cattle field, full of skittish heifers.

The trick here was to open the gate, drive the VW in and close the gate, at the same time keeping the heifers from breaking into the meadow. This, of course, took up a lot of time, sprinting back to the car, shooing the heifers, racing through the gate, jumping out closing the gate.

This process was repeated at the next gate which was the turnip field. The heifers were clever – they would follow the VW, kicking their legs in the air, and they never tired of trying to break into the turnips or the meadow.

At the end of the turnip field was the sheep field. I think the sheep had taken lessons from the heifers for they were up to the same tricks.

The last gate led to a field with an enormous bull. He never came near the gate but when he saw the VW he would start tearing up the ground with his front hooves, his head down and his malevolent white eyes pinned on me. However, I'm glad to say he never actually attacked me.

The final gate led into the yard and house. What worried me more than any bull was the awful woman with her hands on her hips who always confronted me in the yard. Eyes blazing she would demand to know why my boss himself hadn't come. I didn't tell her it was because of those damned gates. Eventually she would reluctantly let me look at some moribund animal in the shed, which I suspected had been treated by the owners themselves.

My successor, however, had a shiny bright red new Consul car and the bull, it is thought, saw his own reflection in it and pushed in the side of the car with his mighty head. This same gentleman, fed up with all the gate-opening hassle and the client abuse, took a nice revenge. On his last call, before he left the area for good, he left all the gates open on his way out. There was pandemonium.

Two years later he met his former employer at the RDS show. They exchanged greetings and then the boss said, 'You hoor, you left Mrs Newton's gates open!'

# *The nun*

I HAVE treated animals, mainly pigs and cattle, in many religious institutions. Nowadays, however, a convent herd of Friesians would be the exception rather than the rule, as much of the land has been sold for building, and many convents and monasteries are closed down, due to the decline in vocations.

I was surprised to get a call to a convent which I knew was normally attended by another vet. I reckoned he must have been ill or on holiday.

The atmosphere was not great either. The man who looked after the cows was grumpy, not very communicative. The cows themselves were highly nervous and difficult to handle.

But the strangest thing of all was that there was no water tap in the cowshed, nowhere for washing one's hands. Each time I did a job in the place, Grumpy would knock on the door which led into the convent. The door would open about two inches. He would mumble something.

Eventually, a nun would scurry out with a bucket of water, soap and towel. She would place the bucket on the ground, the towel beside it and the soap on top of the towel. She would then run back in and lock the door. She never looked at me or spoke. Her eyes were downcast all the time.

I wondered why she ran in and locked the door. Did she think I might be in hot pursuit?

I tried to find out about the other vet from Grumpy, but he would mumble something, so I was no wiser.

After six months, I sent my bill to the convent. On my next visit Grumpy told me the Reverend Bursar wanted to see me in the parlour. I took off my wellingtons and combed my hair in anticipation of the lovely tea and biscuits I was going to receive – plus, of course, my cheque.

I waited in the parlour for half an

hour. I wondered was it a mistake, then a door opened and a stern-faced nun appeared. She held my bill at arm's length in front of her as if some abominable smell was emitting from it.

'Is this your bill?' she asked with a frozen hatchet face. 'That's a shocking bill.'

I looked at the bill in her hand. 'Well, I see my name and address printed on it,' I said, 'so obviously it's my bill. Neither is it a shocking bill – the charges are standard charges recommended by the Veterinary Association.

'Furthermore, Sister,' I said, 'I am a professional man: I went to secondary school and university. I resent strongly the manner in which I have been treated here. Leaving me waiting for half an hour is the height of bad manners, not to mention your act about the bill.'

I then brought up the question of the other nun in the yard and the way she never looked at me or spoke. 'The atmosphere here stinks,' I said. 'And I do think you should consider leaping the wall: you are certainly a very unhappy lot. Furthermore, get someone else to do your work in future.'

I stormed out of the parlour.

My cheque arrived the next day. The other vet had, I believe, a similar experience and that was why he left.

# The parrot

ONE elderly vet I worked for in the west had, at one time in the 1920s, worked in an exclusive small-animal practice in London. A collar and tie was mandatory for vets in the practice and dusty shoes would have been frowned upon.

The principal of the practice went away on holiday one summer, leaving Patrick in charge. His first call was to an egg-bound parrot. This is to say the parrot, which was a large multicoloured type from the Amazon, had an egg that she couldn't lay. Patrick looked up his exotic-animals book and found a reference to this problem. The treatment was to insert a lubricated finger into the cloaca and oil the egg.

The woman owner was very worried about her parrot and when Patrick arrived she was much relieved. He assured her he would soon fix the parrot.

First he opened the cage – the parrot deftly jumped out and seized Patrick's cheek in his powerful beak. The pain was severe – when you think these parrots crack nuts with their beaks you can imagine what they can do to a cheek. The blood ran down onto Patrick's snow-white shirt, which was now destroyed. The owner was not in the least concerned about the vet: only her parrot mattered. Slowly Patrick disengaged the parrot from his wounded face and, turning the parrot's beak away with a fist around its neck, got the egg out.

Still no sympathy from the owner. 'How much do I owe you?' she snapped.

Pat got paid and drove straight back to the surgery, where the staff thought he had been stabbed.

I said to Patrick, when he told me about it years later, 'If the owner hadn't been there, what would you have done?'

He said, 'I'd have rung its f—g neck.'

# Peter's pony

I HAVE always had sympathy for a person who owns one cow or one pony, because they usually are so upset when anything goes wrong with their animal.

Peter was an example. He kept the sweet shop in a nearby hospital and he had this pony. It was no ordinary animal: it had won numerous prizes for show jumping and was Peter's pride and joy.

One evening, Seamus, who ran the livery stables, rang to say that Peter's horse had cut its abdomen while jumping a fence.

I went over thinking that all I had to do was stitch a wound. When we put on the stable light, my heart sank – a large loop of bowel was protruding from the cut, which must have been deeper than was thought.

I only had one dose of horse anaesthetic in my bag and I gave it to the animal. He went down very quickly and I got the stable lads to roll him over. I washed the now soiled bowel as best as I could and tried to push it back, but failed.

I then opened the wound further and this time I got the mass of bowel back in–I could feel the bladder as I went in. I pumped the passage with antibiotic tubes which are normally used in mastitis cases. I stitched the wound with strong linen and injected the animal with a large dose of penicillin/streptomycin and an anti-tetanus injection.

Peter arrived in the middle of all this. I recall his white worried face. He asked me if the horse would be all right and I gave him a very guarded reply.

When I came home I looked up my veterinary books, as I was not really a horse vet. Dollard's *Veterinary Surgery* stated that there was a serious danger of death from peritonitis, shock, haemorrhage and tetanus. Later I consulted a colleague who was a horse specialist. He said the chances of recovery were very low.

I was sure there would be a fatal result due to the soiling of the bowel with straw, manure and dust. The following day I returned. I walked along the stables but I couldn't see the animal.

One of the stable lads looked up from his work and said, 'You passed him – he's two stables back.'

There he was eating away. I didn't think it was the same animal. I looked underneath and there were the stitches. I gave the animal antibiotics for several days running, as I was still thinking he would succumb.

He did not, and subsequently went back to his show jumping with renewed success. Peter came to me every Christmas Eve with a large box of chocolates.

# TB scheme

THE Bovine Tuberculosis Eradication Scheme started in the 1950s.

It involved a great deal of detail, and still does. The animals had to be tested to see if they had TB. This means that each animal had to be caught and its breed, colour, age and sex recorded in a field book. The neck of the animal was clipped in two places and tuberculin was injected into the skin, but not before the thickness of the skin was measured with callipers.

The ear was stamped with spiked numbers which showed the herd number, county letter and individual number of the animal. Seventy-two hours later the skin was measured again and the difference in thickness recorded. Then, depending on the measure of increase, a diagnosis was made.

The early days of testing were chaotic. Some farmers thought that the vet first looked at the animals and visually decided which ones had TB (the thinner ones) and which did not.

So when the vet arrived the animals would be out in the field. Cattle chutes were non-existent, so animals, particularly bullocks and heifers, were *caught loose* in sheds.

After a day's TB testing the vet could look as if he had been on a battle field – dirty, bruised and exhausted.

On the second day – the day of reading the test, the cattle were twice as difficult to manage, as their ears were sore from the spiked numbers.

Some animals would have reacted with large swellings. The farmers would slice the swellings with a razor – to reduce the lump. Or so they thought!

Occasionally animals were hidden if the client thought they wouldn't pass the test. On one occasion, I had sent notification to 10 farmers that I would be arriving to test their cattle on a particular date and time. The time allotted to each one depended upon how many animals they owned.

I arrived at the first farm and drove around the rear of the house to the cow sheds. The cows were not there. I could see they had been milked and let out. I knocked on the door of the house. There was no one in. Puzzled, I went to the next place. It was the same story – no one in the house. I wondered if I'd addressed the notification cards correctly or, if the cards had yet to be delivered, as this was a remote region in the west of Ireland.

After visiting six of the farms, all with no one in, I turned a bend in the road. At the next house there were a large number of cars, bikes and tractors parked outside. I hesitated, as I thought there must have been a sudden death, or perhaps a dreadful accident. I left the car on the road and walked in.

The house was packed with people and there was a terrific din. They were all talking and laughing so I reckoned it was unlikely there had been a tragedy. I approached the back door and I said hello to the first man I saw. Almost immediately, I was handed a plate of bacon and eggs.

'What the hell is going on here?' I asked.

'Father Jack is home from Florida,' was the reply. 'And this is a Station Mass.'

No testing was done that day.

On another occasion I went to the Nephin Mountains in County Mayo.

I arrived at the first farm. There was a tiny cottage on the side of the road. It was 9 a.m. At the rear of the home was the beautiful Nephin range with the September sun lighting them up in contrast to the fog and rain of other days. I knocked.

'Wha's that?' said a voice.

'The vet,' I answered.

'You're very early.'

'Well, I did say 9 a.m. on the card.'

'Will you drink tay?'

'Yes.'

He opened the door – he had a shirt and braces on – he put on his pants whilst talking. We drank the tea and chatted about anything and everything.

Eventually I said, 'Now, about the cattle?'

'Here, Shep, go out and get the cattle.'

A black-and-white dog shot out from

under the bed in the corner and went out of the door. There were no cattle in sight.

'Did you ever see a Mass Rock?' asked the farmer.

'No,' said I.

'Well, I'll show you one!'

We walked high into the hills. I was panting when we got to the top and there it was. A large flat granite stone with a crude cross etched on the top. He explained how the countryside could be surveyed for sight of the Redcoats.

We descended, but there was still no sign of Shep or the cattle. However after a few minutes I heard the thunder of the hooves and in they swept into an old roofless ruin at the back of the farmhouse. There were horses, foals, calves, cows and some bulls. They were a wild bunch. I began to think *'How is this man going to catch all these animals by himself? Who is going to stop them escaping while I'm testing?'*

I stood in the doorway. The wild-eyed cattle took one look and the stampede started. They jumped through the door and the windows, over walls and, in a great cloud of dust, they careered back up the mountain. I suppose they had scarcely seen anyone except the owner – in other words they were stone mad!

I still managed to test some of the neighbouring small farms. Some had only one cow and a calf. As there was no industry in the area, neighbour helped neighbour, but none wanted to be involved with the first man's cattle as they were 'single-suckled' and rarely handled.

The postmen, if I encountered them, were a great help with directions. They had to travel enormous distances on a bicycle and at Christmas would try to carry parcels which came from Britain or America. Some of these contained clothing and the American clothes were much sought after. One farmer had an American-style post box with *U.S. MAIL* printed on it.

No postman at Christmas could deliver all the parcels by bicycle, so some people had to wait a long time for their delivery. Eventually, one of the postmen bought a VW van and was able to deliver speedily the much-wanted parcels in one day. There was great delight in the poorer communities. Alas, the postman was suspended by the Department. However it eventually led to giving all postmen vans and to the service we enjoy today.

Occasionally I suppose, in all walks of life, one will encounter people who are, for want of a better word, mad!

Charlie encountered me at Mass one Sunday. 'I have five bullocks and I want to sell them, but they're not tested. What do I do?'

I got him to fill in the appropriate form and shortly the instruction arrived from the Department to proceed with the test. I notified Charlie, who lived with his sister. He had five bullocks tied in and I didn't have much trouble. The animals were huge, having been hand-fed.

I sent the report to the district TB office and one Sunday at Mass Charlie came to me and said, 'Yer a great man – I got the ID cards for the cattle.'

The following year I again tested the cattle and updated the cards by stamping and signing. On the third year, Charlie sheepishly came to me to say he had lost the cards and asked what could be done. I wrote an explanatory letter to the Department and Charlie was given new cards. Again he beamed at me at Mass and thanked me profusely.

Through some error the Department

sent five more duplicate cards but, in the meantime, Charlie had found the lost ones – he now had 15 cards for his cattle.

Next time around, I attempted to take back the ten unwanted cards. Charlie's attitude changed completely. He refused to hand them back, saying that he knew what tricks I was up to.

'What tricks?' I asked, but it was a waste of time as he was getting more aggressive by the moment.

Then I noticed Charlie's sister standing directly behind him in the doorway. She was pointing to her head and mouthing the words, 'Don't *mind him.*'

I took the hint and left. I met her later that year and she apologised. She told me Charlie was now in the mental home!

Another feature of veterinary practice in the west was the fabulous scenery. Places like Killary Harbour, Delphi and Achill. There was so little traffic on Achill that when the dogs would hear the put-put of the VW engine they would follow the car in droves.

I can't remember which post office I made a phone call from. There were cobwebs on the phone because it was so little used.

One Good Friday after a breakfast of two fried eggs, tea and toast, I went, accompanied by an elderly vet (my boss), to test cattle a long way from home. As the vet's sister had a pub in another village, we went there for lunch – potatoes, onions and two poached eggs. When we arrived back that evening, tea at the vet's house consisted of two boiled eggs. I felt funny for some days after and I couldn't look at an egg for months!

I was also vet to an asylum in a large town. The head warder kept cattle on 30 acres inside the high walls.

One Saturday, I came to test some cattle for the warder. I had been wondering if he would be able to get help, this being a weekend. He did find three men to help – and they were just great. I thought they must have been warders. We had great craic during the work.

Pat, the warder, later told me that the helpers were inmates. Two had killed their fathers and the other one had a problem with sheep.

# Poteen

I FREQUENTLY encountered poteen (or illicit brew) in the West and on one occasion in the East of Ireland.

The first encounter was one autumn in a field in Tipperary when I noticed something glinting in a hedge. The leaves were falling off and they had exposed a copper 'worm'– this is a spiral copper pipe used in the manufacture of poteen.

The farmer denied all knowledge of the worm but, after I had assured him I wouldn't tell on him, he relaxed and told me all. He said this location was ideal because the nearest Garda station was many miles away. Also, there was one track to his farm–which was clearly visible from where we stood, and a garda on a bicycle could clearly be seen miles away. Many Garda stations did not have a squad car in those days.

Anyone trying to purchase yeast or golden syrup would be suspect, and most shops didn't keep these substances, at least openly, or they would be suspected of being involved in the manufacture.

Potatoes and barley were the main ingredients for making the brew.

One farmer I knew had just drawn off a bucket of poteen from his still and was walking down the yard when a garda cycled in. They exchanged pleasantries–the garda had only come to remind him to cut thistles and yellow heads.

The farmer had put down the bucket when he saw the garda and walked away from it leaving it standing in the yard. Unfortunately, while they were talking, a horse came down the yard and drank the whole bucket. The garda had just left when the horse dropped dead.

When the gardai raided poteen stills the event would be headlined in the local papers with photos of hatchet-wielding gardai breaking open barrels and pouring the poteen into the local river. This latter

practice would certainly be frowned upon by environmentalists nowadays, and might very well be illegal.

On the border with the North we frequently encountered staggering pigs with a whiff of poteen on their breaths. These pigs would have been smuggled. The poteen stopped them from squealing in the lorry when being transported across the border.

I once saw a local dispensary which was used by a travelling doctor and district nurse once a week. It was filled to the top on that occasion with poteen bottles ready for distribution. Next morning all were gone.

My personal use of poteen was motivated by my friend, John, of the hair-today-and-gone-tomorrow episode. A sore throat epidemic had invaded the small town and everyone got it except yours truly. That is, until everyone recovered and then I got it and how! I felt absolutely terrible.

John made me drink almost a half pint of poteen laced with honey. I took it and went to bed. In the early hours of the morning I got out of bed and hardly felt myself falling flat on my back onto the floor. John heard the bang, got up and held me over the loo, where I seemed to pee for ten minutes! I recovered rapidly after this.

When working on the East coast I knew an area where there were many people from the West who had been resettled on Land Commission farms. I said to my boss, 'I bet they make poteen here.'

'Not at all,' he replied

A month later the Gardai raided the area and a still was uncovered. A man was prosecuted and fined £200, which was a very heavy fine in 1950.

Many years later I met the retired Garda superintendent who had lived two doors away from me in the West back then. He was now living in Dublin. We met in Clerys and went to a nearby bar to reminisce. We talked about many things but eventually we got around to the poteen raids, which he had organised and supervised.

I asked, 'How was it you never raided Bill Summers?'

'Aw God,' he replied, 'sure he made great stuff. Sure it was as good as Jameson!'

# The breakfast

THE CALL came at 5 a.m. There was a cow having difficulty calving. It was a half-hour journey to the hillside farm which was a neat, tidy place with all the signs of prosperity. The shed was clean with plenty of straw and there were two men to help.

It was a difficult case and it took all of my strength to get the huge calf out alive. The men made no comment and just tended to the calf – I was surprised, as usually people would say 'well done', or words to that effect. I put it down to the early hour.

As I returned to the car and commenced washing my boots and rubber apron I caught the scent. It was absolutely gorgeous and it set my taste buds tingling. There was a great tradition in this area of home-cured bacon and in many houses the flitch would be seen hanging from the kitchen ceiling, to be utilised at will.

I had visions of a great mug of tea, the homemade bread and a plate of those luscious rashers. I washed myself slowly while awaiting the call to the table. Nothing happened.

I asked the woman of the house for more washing water as a means of stalling and giving her time to get my breakfast ready. Still no invite.

Eventually I conceded defeat. 'I'm going now,' I said.

'Goodbye,' said the woman and, like a beaten dog – and a hungry one – I drove back to the surgery.

Over the years I found, as many other vets did, that Irish hospitality is not necessarily a nationwide phenomenon. There are some counties where the hospitality is a normal way of life and others, possibly the better-off areas, where it is non-existent.

# The scientist

IT IS well known in veterinary practice that smaller farmers are better payers than the bigger ones. This is probably because they don't want impending debts hanging over their heads.

I got a call one winter's evening to a tiny village in North Galway to attend some sheep. The client's house looked tiny in the fading light. After I had treated the animals the man invited me in for a cup of tea.

I entered the dwelling and met his wife. There were three small poorly-dressed children present. The kitchen was lit by a single bulb hanging from the roof on a long cable. There was a table, chairs and a sideboard but very little else. I surmised they were not very well off. Nevertheless the man proffered some pounds to pay me as payment.

As I drank the tea I noticed a picture over the fireplace of a young man in a graduation gown. I enquired who he was and the woman replied it was their eldest son.

I asked her what did he do and she said he's a class of a scientist. I was very keen to know more and I asked where he was working. The man couldn't remember the name of the place and the woman went to the bedroom and came back with a letter that she handed to me.

The letter was from their son and I was stunned to find he was a deputy director of an atomic research establishment in Britain. The bright young man had scholarshipped his way first through UCG and then further afield. It made me think there is talent everywhere in Ireland, just waiting to be tapped.

# The menagerie

PADDY was a farmer, as well as a vet: he had a farm about a mile outside the town in the west of Ireland. The field at the rear of his surgery had a collection of animals that, for want of a better word, were physically challenged.

The heifer with a cyst on her brain could only graze in a circle. Each morning, a group of us would push her to a new spot to make another circle of cropped grass.

Of course, she had perfect calves. Paddy had purchased her at a low price, and the owner was glad to get rid of her.

Then there was the bullock with a non-identified nervous twitch in one hind leg. Each time he moved, this leg would

leap uncontrollably into the air and down
again.

Another bullock had its heart outside the chest wall, and the heart could be
felt throbbing, as it was just underneath
the skin. Of course we had all kinds of
jokes about broken hearts and so on. Of
course when these animals were sent to

the abattoir to be slaughtered, there was nothing wrong with the meat.

One day, Paddy asked me to bring a small calf to the fair. John, the vet's employee, took the back seat out of the Volkswagen and put the calf in.

We drove down the main street of the town on a very hot day. Due to heavy traffic, I had to brake hard on one occasion, and at that instant the calf was pushed forward with his rear end pressed against my left ear. I felt the hot smelly contents of his bowel on my ear neck and inside my shirt. I had to fight hard not to throw up with the vile smell and it took me a long time to wash everything and myself when I got back to the surgery.

The smell persisted for some time however.

# Warts & all

FRED had two heifers with papillomas or warts. These were relatively common in cattle and other animals – including man. They are believed to be viral in origin. They are usually found in younger bovines and are greyish to black-coloured benign tumours.

Sometimes if one gets damaged, the rest may fall off. This is due to the virus escaping from the tumour, gaining entrance to the body and creating an active immunisation. Alternatively, a vet may remove one, have a vaccine made from it and inject it into the animals.

Many wart infections clear up spontaneously. The warts are usually on the head, chest and shoulders, rarely on the legs.

Fred's heifers had an awful lot of warts, but one beat every record – it was like a large football, just in front of the tail root, and it wobbled from side to side as the animal walked. Something had to be done about it.

Fred got a few neighbours in to help because the animals were quite wild. The shed where we were going to do the job was in a corner of the field, but there was a space at one gable end where they might escape back up the field. Some barrels and a heavy plank on top should stop them escaping if they ran past the open shed door.

I had sedative, local anaesthetic and sterilised instruments ready on a tray before I left the surgery.

The heifers were single suckled, had never been handled and were very wild. Fred and the boys drove them down the mountain; they galloped down, eyes wild, froth coming from their mouths. They shot past the open door and ducked smartly under the plank, knocking down it and a barrel. As they shot past me, I was sprayed with blood. I had a glimpse at a large crater where the 'football' tumour had been, and then they were gone back up the hills.

Fred came panting down. 'We'll try again.'

'No need,' I said, picking up the large tumour out of the muck.

'How did you do that?'

'I didn't. The plank sliced it better than I could.'

I knew if we chased them she would only bleed more. Both recovered from the wart infections subsequently.

One Saturday night I was reading the paper after doing a heavy day's work. The doorbell rang at 9 p.m. I thought it must be a calving case, certainly something urgent. I opened the door, a man walked in, then a woman, another smaller woman, and finally another man. He was carrying a cage. No-one spoke. They stood around the surgery table. The last man in pointed to the budgie in the cage.

'What's the problem?' I asked.

He rotated the cage until the budgie's rear was visible. Then I saw the large tumour. I couldn't see what it was attached to so I took the budgie out and held him with his head cradled in the space between first finger and thumb. It seemed to me a pretty hopeless case. The shock of removal might kill him, and some budgies just die of fright when being handled.

But this budgie was tougher than I thought. While I probed the tumour with my right hand he sank his beak into the skin between my left thumb and finger. Because of the pinching I had to let go.

The budgie flew around the surgery and landed on the man's outstretched hand. The tumour was gone. To my amazement it was in my right hand! It was obviously hanging on by a thread. The expected gush of blood never materialised. It was ready to fall off anyway.

'How did you do that?' said the man, amazed at my skill.

'Oh, it's just a knack one acquires!' I said loftily.

The man paid me and the less-solemn procession wended its way out of the surgery door into the night.

# The widow's legs

MICHAEL was a student with me in college. When we qualified, he went to South Tipperary where he ran a very successful veterinary practice.

Following a car crash, and horrific injuries, he phoned me from his hospital bed and asked me if I would do locum for him until he recovered. I came to South Tipperary and I ran the practice for several weeks. Eventually Michael returned, and he asked me to stay for another while. He would go around with me in the car but he wasn't able to do much heavy work. So I agreed.

We practiced – went out together – on many occasions. There was one place where Michael used to pass by – there was this mountain, and the road was at the bottom of the mountain. Michael told me that there was a widow woman who had a farm right at the top of the mountain. She had no phone so, when she wanted the vet, she would put a red flag on her gate.

Michael frequently passed by this gate during the week. He also told me that this woman had the best pair of legs he had ever seen. Needless to say I was anxious to see the lovely legs.

But nothing happened.

One day we were passing by the gate. I never noticed, but Mike did. 'The widow's flag is up,' he yelled. Gleefully I opened the gate and we drove in.

Up and up, and up and up the mountain a long long way. Finally we came to a yard where there were a lot of cows in a lean-to shed. I stood in the shed grinning, catching Michael's eye occasionally.

When, eventually I heard the footsteps, there she was – The Widow. Unfortunately her skirt was down below her ankles.

As I said to Mike on the way home, she must have heard him talking about The Legs.

# A bridge too far

T IS the Murphy's Law of a vet's life that, if one gets a call to an unknown destination, is always late at night and in stormy weather.

That's exactly what happened one November night in 1957. The address was Tawin. I was in Athenry. I was told to go to the pub in Clarenbridge which was eight miles away 'and they'll tell you'.

I did just that and was told 'Straight on', and those inevitable words, 'You can't miss it'.

After a long drive in blinding rain I met a man with a bicycle. He was walking because the wind would have blown him off his bike. He also said 'Straight on', and on I went.

I saw the STOP sign too late, and then the front of my Morris Minor was in the Atlantic. A wave hit the right hand wing and splashed up on the windscreen.

I was terrified. In a split second I put the car into reverse and, to my intense relief, it responded.

On dry land again I surveyed the white tops with my headlights. I must have come the wrong way somehow.

I turned and raced after the cyclist – eventually there he was, still walking, his shoulders hunched against the gale.

'You sent me into the sea,' I shouted.

'That's correct,' he said. 'Sure

Tawin's an island you're going to.'

'But the waves!' I protested.

'Wait for a minute or two and they'll die down. Then make a dash – it's quite safe.'

Back I went, but first I opened the car windows fully so I could escape if the car sank. I could see the headlines in the local paper – *Body of vet washed up on Aran Islands.*

I entered the sea slowly. Then I saw somewhere ahead a lantern waving from side to side. I felt a lot better. I got across OK and met the lantern carrier.

'I suppose you got a fright when you saw the sea?' he said.

'You can say that again.'

The cow I had come to treat had Redwater disease. This is a tick-borne disease which destroys the red corpuscles. These are passed in the urine hence the term 'redwater'.

Blood transfusion is the best treatment in advanced cases but, with TB rampant in cattle at that time, it was not an option. Because of the loss of blood, bowel movements ground to a halt and, after injecting a substance to kill the disease, rehydratation was the order of the day.

Normally a stomach tube was inserted up the animal's nose and into the stomach and buckets of fluid containing salt, *nux vomica, ammonium carbonate,* and *sodium bicarbonate* were given. Hot ale was also sometimes given.

I made several trips, mostly by day, to this cow. One night I had administered a bucketful of the fluids and, as was the usual practice, I blew through the tube before I withdrew it from the stomach to make sure no liquids went into the lungs. By coincidence, just as I did this, the cow lifted her tail an sprayed the whitewashed wall.

An elderly gent, one of several observers, looked at the wall, then at me blowing the tube and observed, 'I never saw a man blow through a cow before.'

The cow did recover.

Only two years ago, I returned to the scene. Now there's a bridge from the mainland to Tawin.

# *The cow that couldn't pee*

I ARRIVED in the office one morning to be told there was a very urgent call to an address in Ballinderry on the shores of Loch Derg. It was from an owner who said his cow couldn't pee.

I had never heard of such a case like this before so I drove to the place thinking on the way how am I going to deal with this? I drove into the avenue and noted the fine house with yard and stables.

The man standing in the yard had a dickie bow and a short white coat – he was certainly no farmer.

I asked where the cow was. He replied in what I took to be Spanish, and it was clear he had no English. I went to the kitchen door and knocked.

A giggling housemaid opened it – she had no English either.

By this time the man, who was in fact the butler, had noticed the veterinary equipment in my car and pointed to one of the stables. I laughed to myself when I saw the cow – she was trying to calve ! I put on my rubber apron and eventually, after a struggle, delivered the calf.

At this stage a man, whom I presumed to be the owner, arrived in the stable. He was absolutely stunned and overcome with joy. He thought I was a genius and kept saying:

'I say, jolly well done. You're a great chap.' He slapped me on the back. 'Come into the house – you must have a brandy after all that.'

I didn't like to say that I didn't drink, so I followed him into the house anyway. I sat on the sofa in the sitting room which had a picture window looking out onto Loch Derg. He poured out the brandy and then he pushed a delph box towards me, flicking open the lid to reveal a selection of cigarettes and cigars.

I took a cigarette. He lit my cigarette with a Queen-Anne-style Ronson table lighter. The tobacco was black and strong.

We talked about various things. Then he suddenly said, 'My uncle's coming here tomorrow – damn nuisance!'

'Why a damn nuisance?' I asked.

'Oh, he's a Jesuit, and I have to go to Mass every day while he's here. I say, do you shoot?'

'I do,' I said.

'Would you come down here some day? The bloody deer are eating my trees. I'll give you a 303.'

'A *303*?' I was amazed because a 303 is a military rifle. I wondered how he could have got it and its ammunition into the country.

On the way back to Nenagh, between the brandy and the black tobacco, I was dizzy.

Sixteen years later I was in Dame Street and I was passing by Healy's sports shop. In the window there were two magnificent Spanish shotguns, silver mounted and terrific quality – worth at that time about £3,000 each. Spanish shotguns are highly priced and considered the best in the world.

Sadly they were from the estate of my friend of the brandy. He had just died.

I don't remember when I read the

book , *The Man Who Never Was* – probably sometime in the 1950s. It was a fascinating true story about a man who died in Wales in the 1940s. His body was unclaimed and was acquired by the Royal Navy.

The body was preserved and dressed in military uniform with a dispatch case attached, containing documents referring to proposed allied landings in Sardinia and Greece.

Of course the allies had no intention of landing in either place, but were planning to invade Sicily. The whole thing was set up as an elaborate hoax to deceive the Germans.

The body was taken by submarine and lowered into the sea off Spain. A study of currents and tides had indicated the body would come ashore near Huelva, where many ex-pat Germans were living.

It was reckoned that the Spanish would show the documents to the Germans before returning the body to the British Embassy for reburial.

And that is precisely what happened.

The hoax worked like a dream. The Germans were totally deceived. They took several divisions from the Eastern front

and located them in Greece, and sent further troops to Sardinia. The allies landed
in Sicily virtually unopposed.

Of particular interest here was the British
military attaché in Madrid, one Sir Alan
Hillgarth. He had had a remarkable career.
The son of a Harley Street specialist, he
had attended the Royal Naval College at
Osborne and Dartmouth and served as
sub-lieutenant in the Royal Navy during
the First World War.

He took part in the landings at
Gallipoli, and was the only survivor from
his boat. He himself received bullets in the
head and leg.

During recuperation he learned several languages and studied literature. After
the war he attended King's College in
Cambridge.

His subsequent career included
searching for gold in Bolivia, fighting in
Morocco with the Spanish Foreign Legion,
and writing fiction.

His six novels included *The Black
Mountain,* based on his Bolivia experience.
This was praised by no less a person than
Graham Green.

**The Hillgarth home in Terryglas**

Eventually the British appointed him military attaché in Madrid, where he arranged prisoner swaps during the Spanish Civil War, and also arranged the bloodless handover of Menorca, thereby saving a probable 20,000 lives.

The coming of World War Two brought new duties to Alan Hillgarth.

With Ian Fleming of the British Special Operations Executive, Hillgarth devised a sabotage plan, code-named *Golden Eye*, to be used if the Germans were to invade Spain. This was the same Ian Fleming who later wrote the James Bond novels.

Alan Hillgarth was a key player in

the body-ashore hoax, being fully briefed by the British, and spreading rumours to make sure the Germans got wind of the dispatch case and its contents.

However, he is also the man whose cow couldn't pee. I only realised that years later when I read *Operation Mincemeat,* which tells the story of the hoax, and names the people involved. It is based on recently-released papers from the British government.

**Hillgarth's grave at Terryglas**

Alan Hillgarth had settled in Terryglas, Co Tipperary, which is where I delivered his calf, drank his brandy and smoked his cigarettes.

He lived there until his death in 1974. I have visited his grave in the little cemetery in Terryglas church.

# A night to remember

I AM not likely to forget the night of 23 January, 1958. I have checked with Met Office records, and the temperature was indeed minus 10 degrees C. The temperature on the same date in 1881 was minus 19.4 degrees C.

A call came in at 2 a.m. There was a sick sheep on a farm 10 miles away. I knew where the farm was and arrived in half an hour.

'Where's the ewe?' I asked the client.

'Oh, she's in the field.'

'Where's the field?'

'Up the road,' she replied.

The man of the house came with me to the field. There was no gate. We climbed over the stone wall, walked through the

131

field to another stone wall, and there was a herd of sheep.

It was a bright moonlit night and all the sheep were covered in frost. The frost glistened on their woolly backs.

'That's her,' he said, pointing to a ewe.

It was a mystery to me how he knew one from another.

The water I had brought from the house was now cold, and a thin film of ice was starting to form on it.

I said: 'Look, this is no place to have the ewe: she'd be better indoors.'

We brought her back to the car and lifted her into the boot.

Back at the house the farmer's wife had stoked up the kitchen fire and there on the floor I delivered the twin lambs — one was dead. The farmer was happy enough. I administered an antibiotic and left to go back to my now cold bed in the digs.

I was only 15 minutes in bed when the phone rang again. The call was from another village about eight miles away and this time it was a very serious case indeed – a cow with a prolapsed womb.

I drove rapidly until I saw a group of

men with lanterns and torches, waving on the road. I had to leave the car on the road and walk, carrying my gear down an embankment to an open-ended lean-to. There were about six cows tied there and one was recumbent with a large mass of womb behind her. The cow was owned by a widow woman and all the good neighbours had come in to help.

Just as I started to approach the cow, the cow next to her turned around and put her foot right through the womb of the recumbent cow. Heavy snow was now falling with a fairly strong wind. There was good lighting in the shed and this was supplemented by the torches held by the men. I washed the womb carefully and stitched the holes made by the other cow's hoof. In the meantime, the other cow had been removed to another shed to give me room to work – in case she gave a repeat performance. I then administered an epidural to stop the cow from straining.

Now, pushing back a womb is not an easy task as the womb swells due to the arteries pumping blood into it and the flattened veins not being able to return the blood. After quite a struggle, in which I was ably assisted by the men, I got the-womb back. When I went to stitch the lips of the opening I had run out of stitching. I asked someone to direct me to the shortest way to the car, where I had more stitching. He pointed between two sheds. I lifted my rubber apron to avoid tripping and I ran quickly between them. With the snow and ice I did not see the large hole into which I plunged up to my armpits in what was the drainage water from a dung heap.

The shock was horrendous: my boots were filled to the top, my shirt and pants destroyed. I jumped out quickly and squelched my way to the car, returned and stitched up the cow. In those seconds I kept asking myself  – *Why did I become a vet? Was I mad? Why didn't I take that job in the Bank of Ireland, in a nice suit in a warm office, central heating, nine to five? That would have been a lot more civilised.*

The men told the cow's owner what had happened and she came out. 'Take off those boots,' she said, 'and come inside. I have clean clothes – my son in America is about your size.'

She was the owner of a shower and a bath. Oh, the relief of the hot water on my aching, frozen body. She took the soiled clothes away and I put on her son's shirt,

pants and socks. They were all black – he
was a priest in America!

Then – unlike my experiences else-
where, already narrated – the breakfast,
and what a breakfast! Bacon, eggs, black
and white pudding, toast and marmalade.
I was a new man in spite of the tiredness.

It was now a bright but cold day
when I drove slowly back, the men waving
goodbye with quips like, 'Good luck,

Father' - because of the black shirt and pants.

I returned two days' later to return the clothes and recover my own, which the kind woman had washed and ironed.   I discovered that she was the only person in the village with hot and cold running water and a proper bathroom.

It was certainly a night I would never forget.

# The temperance man

JOCK was not your typical veterinary surgeon. It was his appearance that was so different: he was tall, with black hair, thick black eyebrows and a goatee beard... He reminded me of Abraham Lincoln, he wore dark clothes and a kilt on Sundays. He rarely smiled. On Sunday afternoons he taught the children at the Sunday school in his Ayrshire village, and preached regularly on temperance.

I was the white-haired boy because I didn't drink.

Agatha, Jock's wife, was a really lovely person, bubbly and warm, and, aside from six children to care for, she kept a table and cuisine that would have done credit to a top-class hotel.

The girl in the office was an attractive brunette. She was efficient and business-like, but not terribly friendly. Her nick-name was 'Frosty'. Each morning she would have the list of calls ready for the day's work. Most calls came in before 10 a.m., and only emergency calls came in after this time.

The vehicle I was supplied with was an old Ford Consul. The wheels were out of line and, at over 40 mph, the steering wheel vibrated quite a bit.

One morning, after I had got my list from Frosty, I drove out of the yard and up the hill outside the gate. Almost immediately the engine started backfiring and at the top of the hill it stopped completely. I quickly turned the car, and tried to restart it on the downhill run, but to no avail.

I freewheeled into the yard and ran straight into the office. I froze at the entrance, at the sight of Frosty and my boss locked in a tight embrace. Agatha was away with the children, visiting her mother twenty miles away. I quickly closed the door and backed away.

Trevor followed me out, his face redder than a cherry. 'It was a joke, you know', he said hopelessly.

'I don't know what you are talking about,' I answered.

I could see the gratitude in his eyes. We were really close friends after this.

# Frank's bad luck

FRANK wasn't just another client: he was also a family friend. My uncle and his father had served in the army together and were lifelong friends.

Frank was also one client whose luck seemed to have deserted him. To use a well-worn expression, "If he put a duck in a pond it would sink."

Sometimes I wondered if it was my fault, as everything I treated on his farm died. First there was the cow with the prolapsed womb. I had the womb back in the right place in minutes. The cow was dead next morning.

I was shocked because I had put back wombs that were damaged and sometimes soiled with manure and grass, but all the animals recovered. This cow's womb was clean and undamaged. It didn't make sense, as I was very good at replacing prolapsed wombs.

Then there was the dehorning of the bullocks. Cattle are dehorned so that they can fit into a boat for export without damaging each other. They seem to thrive better as well.

That year I dehorned a lot of cattle including Frank's. A week later Frank rang me to say the cattle I had dehorned had maggots in the stumps.

Not alone had I not had a case of this before, but Frank lived in a mountainous area where flies were not as noticeable as in the lowlands. Nevertheless I treated the fly blow successfully.

There were other animals I treated for Frank – I can't remember for what. But the results were never satisfactory.

Eventually I told Frank I thought he should get another vet as I seemed to be unlucky with him. He refused point blank and said he knew I did my best.

Some time later Frank asked me to castrate a horse. It was a beautiful animal and I was full of foreboding. On the day of the operation I boiled all the instruments carefully. I gave the horse his anaesthetic and washed the area thoroughly. I had given the animal an anti-tetanus injection first.

The operation went successfully, and with scarcely any bleeding. Frank was delighted and invited me in for tea. From the kitchen window we could see the recumbent horse. I had given it the anti-dote to the anaesthetic.

After the second cup of tea the horse was still down so I went out and administered another antidote.

In the middle of the third cup of tea I looked out and the horse was gone. Frank and I went out but the horse was nowhere to be seen.

Eventually one of the neighbours spotted the animal in his field. The horse had got so much antidote that he had cleared Frank's perimeter fence in one jump.

After this Frank's luck changed and everything went well for him.

# Berlin

COW POX is a virus disease which occurs in cows' udders. It consists of initially small, red, raised lumps. After a few days a watery substance appears in the centre of the lumps in a vesicle. This ruptures and a scab appears.

The condition can spread rapidly through a herd, and milking can be difficult due to the soreness. Treatment was always difficult: if an ointment was applied, the cow could lick it off and wet grass also would wash it off.

A pharmaceutical firm in Dublin received samples of a new treatment from a manufacturer in, of all places, Berlin. This new treatment was a jelly which was smeared on the udder and hardened very quickly. One week later it could be peeled off like cellophane and the pox would disappear.

Samples were tested and found to be very satisfactory indeed. As I was associated with a pharmaceutical firm, I was asked to go to Berlin to see the manufacturer with a view to doing business.

Berlin at this time was in East Germany and under four power controls. Access was by designated roads, rail or air and, at the whim of the East Germans, any of these could be closed at any time.

A colleague and I went by train from Hamburg – a distance of 110 miles. The weather was bitterly cold. As we arrived a blizzard of snow started.

It was now evening time, so we got a small hotel near the centre. Next morning it was freezing hard on top of the heavy snowfall and getting around on foot was very difficult. After a weary search we still could not find our quarry. I approached a policeman, who looked in a little book and said, '*Ost Zone*'– East Berlin – as he pointed towards Checkpoint Charlie. I can't remember if we got a visa but we did get a bus and, as we drove through the checkpoint, I felt we might never come back.

The bus had to zigzag through heavy concrete ramps designed so that no-one could race in, or especially out. Eventually, we dismounted from the bus and went to a coffee house to warm ourselves.

The snow, and sometimes the stinging, freezing rain, started again as we trudged through the rather shabby streets with lots of ruined buildings.

Suddenly I saw, through watery eyes, the shop with *Robert Rettberg – Apotek* in large letters over the doorway. A minute later my triumph was dashed to the ground, when I saw that the door and windows were boarded up.

In dismay we stood into a doorway to shelter from the icy blasts and I stood on a man's foot. 'Oh, sorry,' I said automatically.

The foot belonged to a *Volkspolizei* or People's Policeman – he had a white camouflage suit over his field grey uniform – in his gloved hands he held his Kalashnikov automatic rifle.

'You are English?' he asked. He seemed to speak good English himself.

'No,' I answered. 'Irish, from Dublin.'

He laughed and said, 'Ach, I hope

one day to go to Connemara.'

This *Vopo* was a really friendly guy –
we chatted amiably for a long time.

At the end of the street was a wall. I
asked, 'Is that The Wall?'

'*Nein*,' he answered. 'That is a
dummy wall. If you get over that you are
in a minefield before you come to the real
Wall'.

He said being a Vopo was just a job:
he did not like the regime and if he saw
anyone running to jump the wall he would
shoot over their heads.

Then he asked, 'You are looking for
Robert?'

'Yes,' I said.

He held up three fingers. 'Robert was
caught for currency fiddling – he got three
years in a camp.'

I often wondered if Robert ever got
out of the camp and what became of his
excellent pox jelly.

After this we went on a short guided
tour and saw the snowy mound where the
Fuhrer's bunker used to be.

We also saw Spandau prison where
the elderly Hess was incarcerated at the
time. The tour also took in the enormous
monument to those Russians who died in

the battle for Berlin. This monument consisted of a huge bronze Russian soldier, 40
feet high, helmeted and carrying the standard short-barrelled machine gun.

While we were there a South African
visitor asked the guide for directions to the
nearest loo. The guide pointed to a small
building about 200 yards away.

As the snow was waist deep, no one
was prepared to wade through the snow to
go to this loo. The rear of the monument
was chosen by many, including yours
truly, as a temporary loo.

As the graves of many thousands of
Russians were all around, this would have
been regarded as a sacrilegious act, and I
learned later would have got us three years
in a labour camp.

Perhaps, we mused on the way
home, we might have met Robert Rettberg!